www.finishinglinepress.com

THE
MAPMAKER'S
DREAM

A COLLECTION of POEMS

by

Bill Meissner

Finishing Line Press
Georgetown, Kentucky

THE MAPMAKER'S DREAM

A COLLECTION of POEMS

Publisher: Leah Maines
Editor: Christen Kincaid
Cover Art: Sam Frysteen
Author Photo: Steve Woit Photography
Cover Design: Leah Huete

Printed in the USA on acid-free paper.
Order online: www.finishinglinepress.com
        also available on amazon.com

Author inquiries and mail orders:
Finishing Line Press
P. O. Box 1626
Georgetown, Kentucky 40324
U. S. A.

Table of Contents

PART FOUR. UNFOLDING THE WRINKLED MAP

For Christine and Nathan,
who lovingly helped me draw the map
and then followed it with me.

PART ONE

DRAWING LINES
WITH GLASS FINGERS

THE MAPMAKER AND HIS WOMAN

He should be working on his maps, but instead
he spends the day thinking that she is the distance between
point A and point B. She is Bavaria, in black and white, Czechoslovakia,
perhaps, in brown tones, the mountains and rivers
placed just so, the land falling and rising
exactly according to scale.

The paper his fingertips touch is dry,
not like her—such fertile land rolling with meadows and ponds.
Whenever he thinks of her, he thinks of
a pinnacle atop peaks, a valley lush with valleys.
Lately she's traveling to nearby cities, to flower markets, museums
with paintings of galaxies,
intersections he can't quite locate.
He's only sure about rural county highways,
each inch equaling exactly a hundred miles.

His job is to measure the world precisely:
nothing on his map except what's actually there—
a river, the scar of a railroad track, a bluff
that causes an angle in the highway,
the blue dirt roads that stitch up the earth.
She's somewhere in that world, he knows: cafes, aquariums, aviaries
where her eyes latch onto soaring birds.
But he stays in this room, the four plaster walls slowly gliding toward him,
flattening him so completely
he could be the thin line between two rectangular countries.

He wishes he could just forget his maps,
with all their lines squirming crazily
as if etched by earthworms, his maps
with the black and red stars of towns
that never light up the paper.

He wishes he could
write a poem about her on the back of his hand,
the looping blue letters

that tattoo his skin rising and falling
with each movement of his fingers.

In the evening, she finally steps through the doorway.
He's still at his desk, an acre
of blank paper spread out in front of him.
She walks close to him, feathers on her shoulders;
she is Bohemia in color—he can sense all the miles
on the soles of her shoes.

Done with your map? she asks, her question startling him.
He wants to tell her how far away he felt from her
when she was gone, but his tongue is dry, a discarded train ticket.
The only words he can think of are awkwardly pronounced cities:
Istanbul, Mazatlán, Kuala Lumpur, Dusseldorf.

At first their conversation is circular,
concentric, like the azure lines
that indicate the depth of an ocean.
He wants to tell her that she is that body of water, but the names of places
are still caught on his cracked lips:
Budapest, Xpu-ha, Punta Cana, Salamanca.

When he stands and faces her, he realizes
what they have between them
is a map that, no matter where you follow it,
leads to the same place each time:
There, in its center, you'll find two people,
waiting near a small intersection.
Two people, standing on uncharted ground,
staring at each other, their eyes understanding
that they are the shortest distance between two points.

THE GHOST OF MARILYN MONROE SPEAKS IN THE
HOLLYWOOD ROOSEVELT HOTEL

Have you seen me in the

mirror? I loved the breeze from the subway grate that lifted my skirt
to my waist, loved the cool billowing
as that white pleated skirt rose and rose
like a mushroom cloud and I half-tried to push it down
while a million men's eyes—a little embarrassed but still looking—

stared at me.
I wanted men to memorize every inch
of my skin so they'd remember me,
so that I'd always come alive inside their minds,
balanced on a grate and laughing seductively,
train after subway train making the sidewalk shudder beneath

my white heels.
I always yearned for their eyes to follow me like camera lenses
everywhere I went. I wanted to collect their eyes,
keep them in fishbowls in my bedroom like so many glass marbles.
Look at me, I always said, *look at me look at me look at me.*
I still try to say it, on the stairways of the Roosevelt Hotel, but
my lips can't

find any words.
I feel translucent now, like the wings of a moth with all the dust worn off.
I'm nothing more than a swirl of those lace curtains
when the window's closed.
These halls are too dim, the burgundy carpeting too thick.
I hate the way the bellboys walk by me, speaking in muffled tones.
Sometimes I appear in the old mirror in the lobby: a maid, cleaning the
glass in slow circles, notices a sad blonde in the reflection. Turning,
she sees no one is
there. Late at night in the hallways,

I want to whisper in the ears of men
who stroll nonchalantly past me, I want to scream at them.

I want my pleated white dress to billow upward
like a blooming flower, some A-bomb cloud they can't ignore.
But they never seem to hear me.
To them, I'm just a sudden odd draft in this hallway,
a faint, smoky scent of exotic perfume.
For a moment, they might wonder where it came from, and then
turn to look back into their girlfriends'
flawed faces.

THE GROUNDSKEEPER'S TEENAGE DAUGHTERS

We are the dry ones, the ones who grow weak
in faded pastel dresses, even though
we sit near the window.
Why doesn't he water us as he does his lawns, cut just right?

He stops us with his wire fences that keep us in, keep
the world out like thistles.
No boys for us—our father sees to that.
No parked cars coated with moonlight, no kisses to catch the lips
on fire, no touch of neck or thigh,
no flurry of blushes or
flush of blood red for us.

No—dull green we are, not enough sunlight
or moisture. Quiet we are, not spoken to by our father—
he'd rather see leaves grow from our fingertips
instead of gestures,
vines from our mouths instead of words.

He loves only the ground he mows and mows all day.
Our fields are alive and rippling, but he never notices,
too busy with his weed killer, spraying and spraying
until the patches go bald.

We could say so much to you, father—
about our small yearning swells of earth, our thoughts we keep coiled
like stale, translucent water inside a plastic hose
in the garage. Our secrets
stay secrets, smothered in rolls of sod. Our
dreams, like the blades of a lawn mower,
always circle in one place. So

we grow old before we flower, shrinking as we think:
why doesn't he tend us like his million blades of grass?
And why, when we cry, do we cry tears he wishes
were drops of rain falling
on the parched garden?

WHAT I LOST ON THE WAY TO THE CIRCUS: THE LOVE SONG OF SENORITA ROSA

When I was eleven, I was in love with Senorita Rosa.
A rope dancer from Mexico, she twirled on a thick purple rope
high in the big top, her sequined leotards spinning
faster and faster
until they turned a translucent pink,
the motion so quick
and graceful it could make the whole world dizzy.

Those Saturday afternoon shows at the Circus Museum,
her assistant Rico circled her, and she rotated
like the fast-moving hands of a clock, sending me
forward to the day
when I would grow my first whiskers
and whisper secrets into her ear as we sat in her aluminum trailer,
gazing at the two fuchsia flowers growing from the window box.
I didn't know what kind they were—
all I knew was they opened their luminous petals each morning
as I rode my bike past on the way to school,
then closed them at dusk as I rode back,
the buttery light from her small window falling
in a square on the gravel in front of me as I glided through it,
my thin Schwinn tires never kicking up dust.

For her final act, spinning wildly, she held on by just her teeth
while chunky tourists in the grandstands gasped. But I
just smiled and nodded at her from the front row, certain
I was seeing the woman who would someday love me back, certain
she could still see me in those blurred bleachers that circled her.
I believed that someday, I'd bring her safely back to earth—
she'd slide down that long velvety rope
without burns on her wrists or ankles.
My muscular arms would grasp her by the waist,
lower her gently
to the sawdust earth.
I'd cradle her flushed face,
tell her she'd never have to climb

into the high air of danger again.

Near the end of summer, as I left the candy store,
Senorita Rosa strolled past.
I couldn't believe how much older she looked—
the bright spotlight had erased
            those etched marks next to her almond eyes, those
            tightrope lines tracing her forehead.

I smiled at her, but I felt my insides swirling when
she didn't seem to recognize me at all.
Smudged mascara weighing down her eyelids, she just stared
beyond me to the battered Buick idling on the street,
a blue exhalation of exhaust curling up,
Rico's shadow waiting inside.

That night I pedaled hard toward her trailer, angry at her
for letting me see the desert of her face up close.
I rode back and forth in the alley, gravel popping
beneath my bike until I stopped
in the square of light, my skinny body winded,
tires beneath me losing air.

For one last time, I imagined myself in Rosa's trailer—
sitting across from her at the narrow black-and-white tiled table,
the faucet dripping insistently into a yellowed sink
as she exhaled *hola* and then my name.
I'd feel suddenly dizzy as I'd stand and
lift my arms toward her, anxious to
whisper to her, anxious to cradle
her face in my palms, anxious
to touch, just once before they
fell, the soft petals
of her cheeks.

LETTER BY LETTER

That morning of my tenth birthday, I expected
a game, comic books. Instead,
my father lowered an American Heritage Dictionary
into my open palms,
told me he'd give me a small allowance
if I'd learn the definitions from A to Z.
I felt the weight of the book, its embossed leather cover
holding in those 225,000 words.

Caught in the middle of Iowa,
I knew nothing of aardvarks or zzyvas.
So each night, instead of watching TV,
I leaned close to the gold-leafed pages,
studying definitions that often eluded
me, meteors that glowed a few seconds
in the dome of sky before they faded.

I can picture him now, after work at the used car lot,
his beige dress shirt creased like the lines in a county map.
He'd lean back on his La-Z-Boy in the den,
paging through the latest *National Geographic,*
marveling at the ancient mariners who navigated by the stars.
As a young man, he dreamed of jumping on a freighter
to ports in Anchorage, Buenos Aires, Caracas.
Instead, he got a steady job. Instead,
he wanted his son to learn the world,
letter by letter, and then
go there.

Months later, I gave up at F.
I even skimmed some of the blurred pages
just to get all the way to that failure,
then slid the dictionary into a mute dresser drawer.

Dad, I'm sorry. The universe was just too big for me
and I grew away from those words.
But I'm finding them now, years later, for this poem.

Here they are: each one
like the light from a small, distant
star, finally reaching the earth.

THE THINGS YOU CARRY WITH YOU
(for the Scar Therapy Recovery Group)

You all carry something with you. Admit it:
you carry a moon-shaped scar from falling
the amazing distance from bicycle to pavement,
a red line on your knuckle from the scissors
you never knew were sharp as the tip of a star,
a bump on the head from trying to climb to the thinnest branches until the earth
pulled you back.

You carry a piece of gravel in the soft skin of the elbow
from an unexpected tumble. You carry a pebble beneath your cheek—
when you look in the mirror, its small knob
seems the size of a bowling ball.

Confess it: you carry these things, and you carry more—
the graphite ghost of a pencil lead, like a period beneath your palm.
Some carry knife blade tips in their shoulders, pins beneath the skin of their hands,
rusty nails that should be holding
a shingle down, the flattened noses of bullets, the scraps of
shrapnel like iron canaries trapped inside rib cages.

Others carry scars from what's been taken away:
a mole, an appendix, a spleen, the knot of a tumor, the heart.
Some carry black holes that keep pulling them in, pulling them in.
But most carry scars from something they keep:
some carry watches they thought they'd lost, the second hand
still faintly ticking beneath the skin of their wrists.
They carry loads of fine sand from an hourglass.
Some carry shovels, but don't know how to use them.

Others carry dull keys, suitcases, a car door
that suddenly closed on their wrists.
Some even carry the entire car inside them,
the chrome and sheet metal that reared up
as if in surprise when it met an oncoming truck.

Some carry the whole flawed earth inside their chest

as though it were a chipped marble.

Then there are those who carry an unwritten poem—
a weight heavier than stacked stones, deeper
than any carved scars.
The unspoken words cry out to carry you:
they call all the way to your deepest corners
where nothing else can reach,
then wait for an echo.

MY FATHER, STALLED ON THE COUNTY ROADS

He always thought the highway was a place to dance.
But no, it held him still.
He wanted to hold my mother there, to sway back
and forth to Benny Goodman or Duke Ellington on the car's radio.
Instead he held the steering wheel
gently but firmly in his hands, feeling
the treads of the tires below him
thinning mile after mile.

He thought the highway was a place to dance,
but it was just a place to haul the salesman's samples
stacked in the trunk:
bronze banks in the image of Ben Franklin,
shiny fliers for washers and dryers,
small, silent gray boxes of Zenith hearing aids.
Those years, he wanted his customers to save for the future,
to have clean clothes, and to hear the subtlest sounds,
like the slow movement of stars in the night sky. All he heard

on those ninety-five degree days,
when nothing could coax the sky to rain,
was the sound of the dry Iowa afternoon
sighing through the half-open window of the Rambler.
All he heard was the flat voice of the road, telling him:
Come on, why are you slowing? Just accelerate.
Before you know it, you'll drive all the way around the world.

He never got that far. His only trips
were short distances to places no one ever hear of:
Algona to Pocahontas, Okoboji to Spirit Lake and back again,
as though a chain was attached from his bumper to
their dust-swirled Main Streets. He never got to
dance on the center line beneath a sudden rain shower,
his arms wrapped around my mother, the soothing notes
of clarinets and piccolos coaxing
their graceful steps on softened licorice asphalt.

Instead, some days, he stood alone on the shoulder,
his wing-tip shoes crackling on loose gravel,
his fedora tipped back, the hood of his car raised,
as he watched the radiator's hissing steam
rise for a few seconds, a tiny cumulus cloud
evaporating in the wind.

A DAY IN THE LIFE OF A CARNIVAL PRINCESS

Working the **Pop-Em** booth, Ariel can't stop watching the Kamikaze ride
that swings its caged couples high, then dives
straight for the earth, then back
to the clouds again. They survive. They always do.
Dreamers, they are,
like her, a sixth-grade girl just waiting for something to rise, or crash.

Mornings her mother shakes her awake at 8 a.m. in their
aqua and silver aluminum trailer
that never quite gleams in the sun. She wakes
to the taste of deep fried cheese curds. The taste disappears
soon enough, like everything else. She's from a family of
magicians. Her father did a vanishing act, quick and
seamless as any Harry Blackstone.
After that, her mother covered her face with fake veils the color of happiness.
Every day Ariel volunteers her skinny eleven-year-old body
for *The Amazing Child Sawed in Half* trick,
and each time she still comes out whole, almost. She always does.

Only four more weeks until school,
four weeks to con the strollers to toss darts at balloons
for a chintzy fluffy toy that squeaks.
Next summer she'll be hawking
this wood cage again. Break
one balloon and you win a keychain. Two
gets you the second row: a sad set of unicorns, out of air,
strangled at the neck.
Pop three and you get the top row.
Whatever the prize, she knows, you lose.

All afternoon tattooed teen boys in tank tops impress their girls
with their sharp aim. The girls, mouths smeared with pink giggles,
don't know what hit them, little darts deep in their chests.
They play and play for the grand prize of stuffed pandas and ponies.
She hates to tell them there's only sawdust inside.

Near closing time, the strings of firefly lights flicker, blink and flicker.

Hey, people, three for a dollar, she calls to stragglers,
flips a dart to demonstrate,
the balloon exploding
with a gasp, a direct hit. She never
misses, not after years of practice, the red shred hanging
like a deflated heart. She knows that's how easy
it is. Pop a balloon, pop a dream.
Across the muddy midway, the Kamikaze swings
one last set of screamers
straight toward the ground. Somehow
they survive. They always do.

MORNINGS NEAR THE END OF WINTER

Winter mornings, she says she likes to chip the thick layer of ice
from the sidewalk with the heel of her leather boot,
and he says just let it melt—it'll be gone in a day or two.
No, she says, shatter the ice, bring your heel down sharply,
send the translucent puzzle pieces dancing across wet cement.

He says let your dreams settle a little after you wake—
they won't scare you, and they're easier to forget that way, and she replies
no, describe them, tell them right out loud
in the dark room, even if no one is there to hear you.

He says let midnight be midnight and she says
let it be an hour before dawn, if you want. If you want, let it
be an opaque river you can swim down, the glacier somewhere upstream
steadily feeding it. He says the water's moving way

too fast, I'll drown, and she says no, just go with it, let
it carry you. The faster it rushes, the
more buoyant you'll feel, and the sooner you'll reach the
glistening curved rim of the
waterfall, from which the sun rises. You say

you'll tumble down that waterfall and be lost
in the crush of churning water at its base.
Don't worry, she replies, it's no more than the light mist that rises
when you peel the skin of an orange. At breakfast

you peel the skin of an orange, and
outside, her heel clicks the ice like a metronome, clicks
like the sound of a wristwatch
when you press your ear to it. Listen, she
says, listen to these words, listen
to the sound ice makes as it breaks, as it melts, as it
slides across the warm world.

TEENAGE BOY, BAD AT FLOWERS

Maybe I smelled too many at funerals as a kid
while a great aunt or uncle's pale face floated on a satin sea in a casket.
Maybe the color of those flowers disturbed me when
I walked home alone from school—
too bright, too loud, too doted on for a quiet boy.
I never knew what I felt, so I didn't say much. Maybe

I picked one for a girl once and she asked me what kind it was.
I opened my mouth dumbly
the way a crocus opens its mouth at the first streak of dawn, or
the way the rusty trash barrel opened
when she threw the flower into it. Whatever,

at seventeen I let myself become bad at flowers—
begonias, nasturtiums, irises, lilacs, honeysuckle, dreaded pansies—
my tongue stumbled over the names.
I never learned one from another,
though my mother always tried to teach me as she happily ushered me
down the endless rows of her backyard flower garden.

To me, flowers were just things that grew from bud to bouquet,
surprising the world with eye-watering emotions—
those petals of feelings inside myself
that I always thought about plucking
but was too afraid to name.

WHY I DIDN'T WRITE THAT POEM YOU ASKED FOR

I'm sorry, but I've lost the poem I was meaning to write.
I never even wrote down the first letter.
I was in a car somewhere, a question-mark of exhaust rising behind me,
headlights, like flattened moons, pushing back the layers of night.
Or maybe I was walking in an abandoned neighborhood
when the poem came to me. No, I think I was
swimming, the water rippling around my webbed fingers.
Perhaps I was sleeping when it slipped away like vapor from a chimney
into the sky's blue mouth. I must have
whispered one or two lines before I woke
and forgotten them.
I'm sure they were the best syllables I've ever tasted,
so flowing and mellifluous, words
that would have crystallized the beauty of the world
as poems so often do, but I lost them, one by one,
as my eyelids fluttered and they tumbled, like polished agates, off
the edge of a cliff.
I wanted you to hear those words, to roll your tongue around them,
to know their deep-down sweetness.

But now that I think of it, I really was in a car when I
lost the poem. I was driving alone somewhere, and looking for you
in the passenger's seat beside me.
It was a curved or straight highway, as I recall. I was headed
to a diner, perhaps, or to a motel we once visited
where tubes of neon lights hum and buzz,
and then I came to the blinking red light at the intersection, and
wasn't sure where to turn.
I had such a good ending for it, then, until that light
hit me in the face like an oncoming truck and spun my car
in a pirouette, the screeching tires leaving two gray lines,
two thick pencil marks trying in vain to spell
that illusive first
word.

PART TWO

BORDERS: IN SOME
OTHER COUNTRY

THE PROPAGANDA EXPERTS REWRITE
HARRY HOUDINI'S EULOGY

We thought we'd bury him in a casket, his legs and arms
caressed by his favorite handcuffs.
We thought we'd seal the cover, then wrap chains around it
and padlock them shut so we were certain
nothing could get in
or out.
We wanted to stop everyone from thinking of him,
that wily showman, full of hidden keys and picks,
always breaking free no matter what.
We wanted to stop them from thinking of his Chinese Water Torture cell—
those thoughts kept breaking that glass and
letting the water run out.
After all, no one knows this better than us:
if you don't think of a rainstorm, there can be no flood.
If you don't think of a spark, there can be no fire.
We wanted to put shackles on everyone's brains
so no one would picture him again,
being lowered in a locked wooden chest
into the gray skin of the Detroit River.

Please listen to us. We trace only straight lines.
We state only the facts: We measure the borders of a country,
count how many rounds there are in an M16 rifle.
All we wished for, really, was this:
for that which is captured to stay
captured, for that which is wrapped in chains to stay
wrapped in chains until we decide to let it out.
All we wished for was for what is dead to stay dead,
our soldiers posed next to the body
that we're sure will never rise from the dust.
We want our words to encircle the whole world
the way a python's intestine surrounds the softness of a rabbit.
Our words say *yes*, or
they say *no.* No interruptions,
please. Please
no illusion, no magic. We don't want Harry's forehead to

break through the surface
of the river, stunning the crowd to gasps and applause.
We want no mysteries or speculation, only
what we can hold—like gold coins—in the palms of our hands.
Our purpose is not to entertain, or amuse, or to hide a key
that will open a hundred rusty locks.
Our goal is to take any thought we don't agree with and keep it
quiet, bury it, hold it inside the straight jacket of
our minds for a long time
until it is silent, and truly ours,
a seed squeezed to nothing by the darkness.

SONG FOR THE REFUGEES

—After hearing that 92 Cuban refugees were turned away
from the shore of Key West one weekend in December, 2016

The huddled rafters close their eyes,
have buoyant dreams
of warm café con leche, its soft tan foam kissing their lips. Dreams
of lying in their beds on solid ground, the dry raspy sound
of guiro insects serenading them. Dreams
of steamy clubs where they danced with lovers,
bongos and conga drums and marimbas
beating in time with the steady rhythm of

their hearts. They wish they could lean into a rumba now,
but they don't dare: their hands
cling to thin frayed ropes, their ankles lashed to
makeshift inner tube rafts that save them from the cold liquid darkness,
the nightmare

sharks. Hungry, they are, these rafters—
not just for rice, beans, and pulled pork,
but for that other thing: a word
sweeter than mango or cane or the chocolate from cacao,
a word that tastes like freedom

on their tongues. They know their futures are out there:
but like a shimmering mirage in the distance,
no matter how long they paddle, it always
seems to pull farther and

farther away. At the southernmost point in Key West,
cruise ship tourists turn their backs
to the ocean, take flat-footed photos of their

Tommy Bahama smiles. The rafters spot land in the distance,
a thin green disk that appears, then disappears on the surface.
They paddle hard, hoping
at last to finally touch bare feet onto dry land.
And though their bodies are exhausted,
though there is no music yet, they know

they will somehow begin to

dance. And
dance. And dance.

WHAT THEY REALLY WANT

What we want is to step over
the border and give our nearest neighbor
a black eye.
What we want is to gather up our rival countries like cards,
to stack them in a deck,
to shuffle or bend them whenever we wish.

We do not want trivialities, like hands holding other hands,
or a soft touch on the face, or peaceful encouraging voices.
We want our words to slap, to shout, to break knuckles, to cut the skin.
We want our words to weigh
down all other words, to suffocate them.

What we want is the power to press a
button and turn the lights out on a whole continent.
But what we want most
is to launch a missile that,
with its sharp nuclear warhead, will
stab the earth as if it were poking out an eye, blinding it
for once, and for all.

THE CAR TROUBLE

—A man with car trouble is arrested after shooting five rounds into the hood
of his Chrysler "to put my car out of its misery."
—*CBS news*

He loads up his .380 caliber semi-automatic, strolls
out to that 1994 LeBaron on his driveway,
leans over the hood and whispers soft threats to the front fender.
He jumps behind the wheel one last time and cranks the ignition.
The engine grinds and grinds as he rocks forward and back, forward
and back like some zoo gorilla in a glass cage, his eyes sinking deeper
and deeper into his forehead,
his rear end worn to a shine.

Of course the car won't start and won't start, no matter how many times
he digs the key into the steering column.
So he sits there, fuming, stares
through the gravel-bitten, dust-caked windshield and tries to
think for a minute.

Ever want to do it? Ever want to plug that bright neon sign, hovering above
you in the night sky like a false galaxy?
Ever want to shoot the new skyscraper that blocks the view of the lake?
Ever want to shoot the Garden Weasel?
Ever want to blow away a can of Static Guard?
Ever want to blast some Food Channel cookies, to watch the
dough splatter the studio so the chocolate speckles the walls like flies?
Ever want to shoot a newspaper, those smudged pages
filled with all that bad news?
Ever want to plug a Hair Club for Men toupee?
Ever want to line up America's Top Model's makeup bottles
on a fence post, then pick them off one by one?
Ever want to open fire on your TV, the way
Elvis sometimes did?
Ever want to pretend you're some dictator,
tape a map on the wall, pick a country,
and then fill it full of lead?
Man, you could tear it to shreds within a matter
of minutes, like those targets at the carnival shooting gallery

where you never won a stuffed bear. Ever get so angry
you could wipe out a whole country?

He cranks the ignition one final time. When it doesn't turn
over, he strolls to the front of the car, lifts his gun,
and squeezes the trigger, sending a bullet into the hood
right where the carburetor's heart should be.
He waits a few seconds for the LeBaron to plead a little with him—
maybe a quick flash of the orange signal light, a sudden gasp from those
two hundred-dollar tires that never knew where they were going.
Instead, the frozen chrome grille smiles at him.
So he fires another round, then another,
the pale yellow hood dotted like enameled Swiss cheese.

After the execution, he lifts the hood to inspect the damages.
Peering inside, he expects to see some subtle sparks, some oil spurting
from the arteries of this obsolete beast, a faint hiss of smoke,
some green tears of radiator fluid, at least.
Instead, nothing—just the big American engine,
covered with grease like it always is,
just the alternator wires, still curved like black rainbows.

And the only sound he hears is his own whimpering,
his own clear tears splattering on the motionless fan.
He still holds the set of keys, clenched so tightly
in his fist they'll make a red indentation in his palm
even after he drops them to the asphalt
and innocently tosses his hands to the sky,
like someone who knows they're about to be arrested
though they're not sure of the charges.

THE BARBIE REVOLUTIONARIES

In the 1990s, an activist group broke into the Mattel factory and
"switched the voice boxes of 300 Barbie Dolls and GI Joes"
—*Boston Phoenix*

How do you feel, Teen Talk Barbie, now that you can say
"Let's go get em!" instead of "Math is hard?"
Do your slim arms and spindly legs feel
stronger and steroid-enhanced? Do you feel like you could punch
your way out of the clear showcase of your box?
Do you have the unexplainable urge to organize a commando raid
on the factories of American Girl dolls, to destroy them
before they reach the end of the assembly lines?

Equal rights, Barbie: now you can aim an M-16 at the enemy, too.
When the five-year-old girls in *My Little Pony* t-shirts
see you spring out of the box with that
black and green camouflage paint on your face,
how loud will they scream?
And how will their confused fathers react, staring at your
anatomically perfect body sheathed in a scanty dress,
when their daughters pull the voice box string and you growl:
"Dead men tell no lies!"

And Joe, does it puzzle you, why you suddenly
think about slipping on pink fatigues? Or when you picture yourself
browsing through a rack of prom dresses?
Do you feel your testosterone-starved triceps begin to sag?
Stacked with your platoon in cardboard barracks on factory shelves,
you used to dream of bullets and blood,
but now it's only lipstick cases and rouge.

Little boys in Zubas, poised in backyard forts
with plastic guns and mini-grenade launchers
will be permanently scarred by you, Joe, when you command:
"I like to go shopping with you!"

Barbie and Joe, how far will your voices carry?
In the next decades, there'll be Baywatch Barbie, Malibu Barbie,
Lingerie Barbie, Astronaut Barbie, and if you study really really hard,

maybe even Math Barbie.
And Joe, for you there'll be
Desert Storm and Desert Strike and Operation Enduring Freedom—
you've got plenty of fight left in your always-clenched fists.
You'll have smart bombs and night vision: there's always
a whole new threat waiting out there for you to destroy.

But for now, Barbie and Joe, you just lie
behind cellophane windows
until the tiny urgent hands, desperate for your model,
open the flaps and lift you out.
Then you'll smile at them with pre-formed plastic lips,
just waiting for them to pull the string on all that silence.

THE SEARCH

—In 1907, Walt Whitman's brain, donated to science, "slipped out of
the hands of a laboratory assistant, broke into pieces, and was discarded."
—*Walt Whitman Quarterly Review, Vol. 20, 2003*

"I celebrate myself...For every atom belonging to me as good belongs
to you."
—Walt Whitman, *Leaves of Grass*

Before they shattered, where did those dusty synapses lead?
Did those scientists walk down the same roads you strolled on, Walt,
celebrating drums and ships and cradles, wheels and peaks and oceans?
Did they find the cerebellum to be bright
and electrified, the way you wandered through the darkness of the
1850s and found the body electric?

Did they discover, within those passageways, why you wanted to write
version after version of that same book, always longer, expanding
like ever-widening ripples, as if America was a still pond,
and you'd just thrown a stone into its center?

Did their microscopes spot the lonely love of a great grey poet,
still sparking between the neurons?
A few faded green leaves crumbled inside the cerebrum?

A hundred and seventy years later,
what more do we know about America, Walt?
The country is smaller, fitting on one computer screen, one
faded map we fold and keep above the visors our cars.
We're still not sure where all those branching lines pull us.

You could never have imagined skyscrapers and flying machines and
automobiles sucking the earth dry from the inside out.
If you wandered our streets now, Walt, you might write:
        O Internet America! O Ipod DVD SUV America!
        O I-phone web cam text message twitter snap chat America!
        Where are you now? Why can't you ever talk to me face to face?
        O stupid science! The lights go out and go out and
        go out on our country, and we're veiled in a funeral shroud.

Still, the same cloud-haloed mountains you looked upon are there, Walt.
The same gouged canyons painted red and brown, the same
tattered soldiers sighting their rifles on each other, the same lilac bushes
sprouting in back yards, but now their sickly-sweet purple flowers
rest in vases beside our jumbo flat-screen TVs.

It's no use searching for you, Walt, in those
pieces, broken and scattered like a dropped China plate.
All along we should have been strolling across a field and
looking for you beneath our boot soles,
where the April leaves of grass flatten—just for a moment—
before they spring back again.

WHEN THE WAR VETS RETURN

They have only one request: Don't talk
about whether or not the war is good or bad.
So when they return,
     we talk only about the trees, the elms,
the green umbrellas that fill the sky above our houses,
protecting our children from storms.
     Talk only about the begonias in the back yard,
like the ones tended by the soldiers' wives day after day
as they stoop over with copper watering cans
that pour out a stream as clear as their wedding day.
     We talk only about the way their wives wipe the mud
from their feet as they step, barefoot, back into the empty house.
     At night, they dream of walking down a sandy road
toward a distant desert, the mirage of water spreading across it,
creating what should have been a lake, but wasn't.
The wives pause at the lip of that
lake, gaze out and see their husbands,
dressed in fatigues, lying in a small wooden boat,
waving at them as they float toward the far shore.
The wives call out to them with a small word or two,
but aren't sure if they're
heard or not.

Let us say, then, that the war vets' one request is fulfilled.
     We will not talk about the war, whether it's good or bad.
     No opinions here, no opinions.
     If someone *does* dare to talk about the war, we'll ignore those words,
send them away, past the fading green lawns of our
back yards, waiting like sponges, to soak up a rainstorm.
     We'll send the words to other towns, to cities, where
at three a.m. in the all-night cafes, patrons turn their backs
to the black and white hiss
of small televisions propped in the corners.

     We'll banish the words, exile them
across the state lines to our own deserts,
Arizona and Nevada and Death Valley,

those American lands we never knew were so dry,
and yet so close to home.

   The words will travel to those lands, to a parched basin
etched with lines like the cupped palm of a huge hand,
a hand which will open for the words,
letting them pool for a moment into its hollows, and then
close on them slowly,
as if they were never spoken at all.

POETRY CLASS WITH TEENAGE GIRLS AT
THE SUICIDE LOCK-IN UNIT

1

The girls can't keep the sea shells I gave them to write about.
Sea shells can cut, their social worker cautions.
The girls hold the shells in their palms, studying
the mysterious spirals of the flutes and conchs,
the sunset sky spattered on the pale half shells,
the tiny, patient grooves, grown year after year,
always so symmetrical, so perfect.

A poem is like a pond, I tell them, each line like a ripple
that carries to the far shore.
As I read to them in the cramped room, winter's bitter knuckles
knocking on wired glass windows, I feel the small paper cut
on my index finger, wonder
how it got there. I'm sure one girl notices,
and keeps staring at it.

For the next hour, strong words flow
from the sharp edges of their shells.
After class, before an aide collects them,
the girls drop the shells into Ziploc baggies,
scrawl their names across
the transparent plastic in fragile blue pen.

2

At night, one girl lies in bed without sleeping and dreams
of being eight years old again. It's her birthday pool party
at the Holiday Inn with friends.
At this party, there are no salty midnight oceans of pain.
There's no deep and endless blackness—
just inflated pink toys bobbing on soft, shallow water.
A bored mother in pin curlers, eyes fixed on
her *Soap Opera Digest*, mutters:
"Don't go near the far end, girls.
Stay where you can touch bottom."

But she doesn't listen. It's only when
she's near the deep end she
realizes she's not a good swimmer.
Tipping her head back, she gasps for breath,
cups the water, pulls at it in a frantic dog-paddle.
She paddles and paddles,
pulling the years toward her until

she's seventeen again,
paddles and paddles as if it were that easy
to keep herself afloat,
as if it were that easy
to make all those purple cut marks
on her wrists blur and
blur until they finally
disappear.

A FEW WORDS ABOUT GUN VIOLENCE: VIEW OF THE EARTH THROUGH THE *DSCOVR* TELESCOPE

From a million miles away, it looks too blue:
perfectly rounded, haloed with graceful spirals of cumulus,
its continents drifting away from each other
like lovers that long to touch again.
But on its surface,
a person lifts a weapon,
cradles it between a thumb and index finger,
contemplates the black hole
at the end of its long, sleek barrel.

The motive is always a little cloudy, yet the incidents repeat themselves:
in malls, in theaters, in dance clubs, in schools, in schools.
No one can explain why. It's something
to do with whatever it is that spins,
so red and angry, inside someone's skull.

There is no sound in the vacuum of outer space.
But here, some days, you can hear it, so close to you,
in the electronics aisle of a Wal-Mart.
Employees in the stock room look up, startled
by a hollow popping sound that reminds them
of a light bulb rolling off the edge
of a shelf.

From a million miles away, the earth looks blue as gunmetal—
it's that same color we see from our back yards
when we tip our heads to the afternoon sky
and stare beyond those swirling clouds
that hide so much pain.

PART THREE

ALBERT EINSTEIN'S
BRAIN

ALBERT EINSTEIN'S BRAIN, DONATED TO SCIENCE

What did those scientists find as they explored the shadows of the gray folds?
Did their fingertips travel at the speed of light?
Did they see time itself caught there, spinning its endless spider web?
Did they find the seed for the Atomic bomb beneath the layers,
a single neuron exploding
into a tiny mushroom cloud that rose and then settled
onto the lab table like a halo of pale smoke?

Or did they find cracker crumbs, some loose coins, a key ring, perhaps—
the same things you might find
when searching behind a seat cushion for something you lost?

All these questions remain unanswered.

People laughed that Einstein couldn't make change at a store.
At the podium for his Nobel Prize speech,
forgetting his socks and shoes, he stood in bare feet.
His blue branching veins could have been
distant galaxies leading to black holes,
but they were just capillaries beneath the translucent skin of pale white feet.

So did those who studied his brain find anything significant—
nerve endings crisscrossed, a cerebrum with fireworks exploding
beneath its surface, a sizzling synapse
sparking into eternity?
Or did his brain look just about like everyone else's—
so gray and ordinary, a shriveling mass that hardened over the years
like a clump of clay you might use
on a desk as a paperweight?

Perhaps one scientist simply scratched his head, as he always did,
his hair puffing out slightly from his scalp.
And after closing the lab, he drove to the 7-11, light years of stars
plastered to his windshield. There he picked up snacks for the evening—

a Milky Way candy bar, a diet drink, maybe. Pop Rocks for the kids.
Then he stood there in front of the staring clerk, suddenly
unable to count the change in his pocket.

TEN SECONDS LEFT IN THE HIGH SCHOOL TOURNAMENT CHAMPIONSHIP: JAMES DEAN SHOOTS THE BASKETBALL TO WIN THE GAME

> Dream as if you'll live forever. Live as if you'll die today.
> —*James Dean*

The game's always tied, just a few seconds left,
and his feet are always tiptoeing along the out-of-bounds lines.
To stop or to go, that's the question. To be
caught in this Indiana town all your life, acting
your way down Main Street, or not to be.
He's just seventeen, and the basketball in his palms weighs
as much as the entire earth. He can hear the
hissing as if it's slowly losing air. *Just don't think about it,*
his coach always said. He dribbles across the court,
glancing for an instant at the red lines
he's been told to follow
when all the time his eyes were thinking green,
green, so he can accelerate from the stoplight.

Suddenly, he's older, not just a kid, as if pausing and holding
this basketball and staring at the hoop, so far away,
has aged him. The muscles in his arm flex,
like when he'll drink that fast glass of beer just east of Eden,
when he'll sit on that railroad flatcar in the cold night air
and hold his head tightly with both palms
to keep it from exploding.

He balances the ball beneath his line of vision,
and the moons on his fingernails glow.
The hoop floats away like a smoke ring
from the cigarette he'll smoke in *Rebel Without a Cause,*
but right now, he hears the crowd
chanting the countdown: 9, 8, 7. The light turns green.
Accelerate: There are always just a few seconds left.

6, 5, 4. The ball rockets from his hands, arcs upward into
into orbit. It flies so slowly
that forty years pass

as it travels the distance of the dark wooden floor
that's convex, like the surface of the earth.
The ball arcs over America, over
everything James will never live to see:
Kennedy—fouled hard in the back of the head—slouching forward,
the deep scuff marks of Vietnam, Armstrong leaping from the moon's
surface and into soft lunar air, off-balance cities erupting.
All James can do now is watch
as the ball reenters the atmosphere and approaches the hoop,
the sparks tailing behind it like prayers. *3,2,1.*

When James wakes, he's 24 already, pulling himself
from a tangle of sheets.
In an hour, he's due on the set for the morning's filming.
He lights a cigarette, lathers his face with clouds, shaves
so the camera will love him.
He stares in the mirror at the dark rings under his eyes
and remembers that game as it was: just ten boys,
five on each side in a little game, shooting an old leather basketball
on a gym floor warped and pockmarked like any other.
Someone had to win, someone had to lose: there are no ties.
Just don't think

about it. Go.
Before he strolls to his silver Porche for the last time,
he rolls up a wrinkled white T-shirt.
With a quick jump shot,
he lofts it across the room.
It lands dead center in the wash basket with a
swish.

1959: BOB DYLAN HITCHHIKES ON HIGHWAY 61 SOMEWHERE OUTSIDE HIBBING, MINNESOTA

He's dancing with the tattered wind.
Though it might look like he's standing still,
he's always dancing with the wind
that scrapes across the open iron ore pits.

Tonight on this roadside there are no cars,
no *Buick 6* roaring past, leaving him behind,
dust devils circling around his black boots.
The night's so quiet he can almost hear
the stones in the ditch begin to hum.
So he thinks of lifting his guitar
from that battered black case and strumming it,
though he hasn't written a note yet.
     He imagines that first song:
Mountains and seas, cannonballs and doves,
aching notes—and the sudden vacuum.
He'll write it some day, he has to believe that:
With Woody Guthrie's ghost standing over his shoulder,
he'll sit down at his typewriter, slide in a blank sheet and
search behind his sunglasses for the ragged poet,
then snap out a verse or maybe sixty-one,
about neon madmen and chief preachers and diplomats
riding chrome horses,
all of them crumbling like statues slammed
by the hammers of his notes,
about Ramona and Jane and Johanna and Sarah,
each of them coming alive for a few minutes
until he crumples the paper in his fist.

    He remembers his old high school—
his Tom Thumb classmates during the talent show,
their boos dropping like lead weights
from their lips to the hard floor.
He thinks about the stage curtain they closed
on him in the middle of a song, trying to suffocate him.
Instead it gave him breath, made him

play the piano even louder to keep away all that silence.

Tonight there are no cars,
no whirr of tires,
no red taillights fading like tired eyes.
He looks down the empty highway,
that asphalt arrow pointing
toward the distant horizon,
and he knows his future is out there,
always pulling farther and farther away
no matter how much he walks toward it, or stands still.

Just before dawn he thinks he hears the stars fading,
their last shimmer making a jingle-jangle tambourine sound.
He stands there in the first blinks of sunlight:
He's a silhouette, the first dark note
of a song that will play
for a hundred years.

THE NIGHT ELVIS SWALLOWED HIS ROSARY

The night Elvis swallowed his rosary it slid down
easily, then tangled into knots in his stomach
as he swayed and gyrated across the dull brown stage,
a slim velvet black and white tornado gone wild.

I got it, he thought, *I got the note, I got the
look,* and he shook those legs,
the ice cube cool kneecaps colliding
like somebody dancing or fighting with themselves.

After the show the doctors watched him dance
across the X-ray machine,
the coil of crystal clearly visible,
his body held suddenly still on gray film for a moment,
not like on *Jailhouse Rock* bopping in that striped t-shirt
or *Blue Hawaii* on a shimmying surfboard, when nothing could hold him
except fifty-million girls and women who, forty years after he's gone,
still have his smoldering face on their purses.

The night Elvis swallowed the rosary
it knotted itself deep down inside: cross and beads, beads and cross.
It got all wound up with Memphis and smoke
and TVs with bullet holes in them and dented silver screens
and black vinyl spinning and the crowds surging forward
just to pull one thread from his gold suit,

and as it rose back up through his throat
it made such a sound,
a song we'd heard a long time, really, but
never really listened to, some teen-aged kid's voice
in our petrified ears: America, your religion is here.

SOLSTICE DANCE AT THE VILLAGE NEAR CHICHEN ITZA

At the moment the sun lifts its red curve of blood
above the horizon and the shadow falls
from the tiled fountain on the plaza,
a thousand years pass.

The children file in, wrapped in Maya reds and whites and golds.
Headdresses erupt from their foreheads; sprays of feathers
flicker in the wind as if trying to take flight.
The brown-cheeked children are sleepy—some wish
they were still lying in hammocks in their thatched huts,
dreaming of green and red parrots and piñatas.
When the piped-in music crackles from tin speakers
the rhythmic drumming moves their bare feet;
the squeal of carved bamboo flutes lifts
their gaze to the sky.

In the distance, thousands gather at the great pyramid
as the shadow of Quetzalcoatl, the plumed serpent, crawls slowly down
the stone staircase. Inside the pyramid,
the mosaic jaguar wakes
beneath the bare bulbs strung from the dank ceiling,
its emerald legs dreaming of running through the rain forest.
In the nearby sacred cenote, the spirits of the drowned
send up sudden gasping bubbles that break
the algae-green surface.

When the serpent's shadow reaches the base of the pyramid
and opens its eyes, the horizon teeters on its edge.
But no one is sacrificed here,
no strings of thorns jab through the tongue, no knives
lift out beating hearts, no rival warriors are beheaded:
just the yellow song of the sun angling on the limestone, just
the children in the plaza, gracefully twirling into a blur.

After the music stops on the plaza,
a Coca-Cola ad blares from a flickering TV
in the corner grocery.

The first busses, bulging with tourists, rock
over the speed bumps
and the children, feet caked with clay,
slowly lift the feathers
that have fallen to the cobblestones.

A LITTLE SOMETHING ABOUT
THE WORLD'S LARGEST BALL OF TWINE

For thirty-seven years he wound the twine around
and around itself—a work of art, maybe, or just
a ball of twine that made his life a little larger each day, just
a man named Francis Johnson
in the town of Darwin, Minnesota, population
too small, spinning yarns about how big the ball could become if he
kept adding to it for years, for the rest of his life,
even.

He collected it from farms, the lumberyard, the post office—places
where that rough, frayed twine really had a use: holding bales of hay
together, keeping stacks of wood slats
straight, making sure cardboard boxes don't open their flaps and
spill everything they kept inside.

Dull, everyone in town said about him, *Dull, and crazy.*
But Francis didn't care:
Soon the ball grew to six feet in height, and
he had to rotate it a little to keep it
from going flat on one side, like a tire losing air.
Let it grow and grow, he thought, let it roll
all the way across this country, put this lonely island of a place on the map.
Let them marvel at it, flocking to Darwin from all over America,
spinning their wheels toward Main Street, gasping
Twine! Twine!

Useless, people said. *It's just twine.*
But Francis Johnson knew
he could make those discarded pieces feel important,
tie them with callused fingers to other useless pieces,
make the uselessness grow into something long and amazing.

2

In the later years he climbed a ladder to reach the top of his
Guinness World Records sagging gray ball of twine.
It was so big it evolved, almost, as if it had a brain of its own.

Sometimes, late at night when he sat near it, he thought he heard
the sound of rain evaporating from it, or perhaps
it was breathing. Thought he heard some muffled words, a faint pulsing
as if something was living in the middle of its core. A reminder
of who he was, maybe, years ago when
he picked up a short length of twine in the barn,
then circled it around his little finger until the tip turned purple.

Just a ball of twine, or a work of art, maybe—
almost symmetrical, but never
quite.

With just one roll, the eleven-ton ball could crush him, though
he knew it would never turn on its master like that. He knew
they'd sit side by side for a long time, his hand caressing
frayed strings. He didn't care what the townspeople
said—he tied his whole life into this one little
planet. As he added each length, he felt
his heart tighten a little, as if it, too,
were made of twine, as if it,
too, were a ball of hidden
knots, as if it, too
would go on beating
without him
as soon as
he was
gone.

HOW OUR TOWN GOT RELIGION

On an August morning when Channel 10 warned of severe weather,
the ball lightning enters
through the open back doors
of our church and rolls down the aisle,
pale and gossamer, like white cotton candy, wisps trailing from it as it spins.

Hovering a few inches above the black and white tile,
it glides slowly toward the altar
as row after row of startled parishioners wake and gasp, speechless
as though they'd just won the Reader's Digest Sweepstakes.
Caught in the middle of his mumbling prayer and
facing gold-leafed statues and the silver cross of the altar, the pastor never
sees it.

When the lightning ball reaches the altar, it
pauses there, hissing a few seconds, as if waiting for something—
some wafers, perhaps, a sip of wine, a confession
from some of the sinners attending
this noon Mass at St. Lucy the Martyr Church today.
Women cover bare shoulders with their palms, the elderly
trace the sign of the cross with frail fingers, and
the ushers feel compelled to rise up from their pews
and warn the pastor and the whole congregation to save them. Instead
they remain still on aching knees,
waiting to see what God or the Devil will decide to do next.

It's then that the lightning ball rolls backwards,
retreating down the aisle, past the rows
of the electrified faithful, and
exits through the heavy oak doors,
seeking the storm from which it came.
People blink their eyes in amazement
as though the huge cracked cast-iron bell in the tower
had just started ringing on its own.

When the pastor turns to his congregation at the end of the service,
he's surprised—and a little flattered—at everyone's awe,

the pink fervor that seems to be burning in their faces,
as if they had just seen the Holy Spirit
push open all the stained-glass windows at once, or witnessed
that crippled man who always sits in the front row,
finally dropping his crutches and, after all these years, beginning to dance.

PART FOUR

UNFOLDING
THE WRINKLED
MAP

TO THOSE WALKING BACKWARDS ACROSS AMERICA

It can be done, but only if you wear the right shoes:
It can be done, if you don't think about
where you're going—just that you're moving
backwards, getting younger step by step,
becoming thinner and smaller by the mile.

When you back up for so long, you lose some things, too:
what a gray hair looks like, how to drive a car, you and your wife's initials
carved beneath the skin of that huge oak tree
that's now just a sapling in some stranger's back yard.
Your first taste of buttered lobster fades. So does
your memory of the beam of a lighthouse cutting the night sky.
Next the ocean itself drains, its rising and falling swells disappear,
and so does its blueness you stared at for a long time, amazed,
and swore you'd never forget.
The cement where, in grade school, you pressed
your handprint smoothes over.
Your memory of how to tie your shoes fades, too;
your ability to add two and two erases.
Then your shoes themselves become useless and fall away,
and you can't remember how to take another step.
You feel yourself being carried around by others, and
then it happens: you no longer can say sentences, you forget verbs, nouns,
and for a moment, before it evaporates like mist,
your first word lingers on your tongue.
You forget the faces of your mother and father,
the brightly-colored fish mobile that circled above your crib,
a plaster hospital ceiling, the tiny pockmarks that fascinated you like stars.
Finally all you have left is one or two final thoughts in your shrinking cranium:
What's that warm cave you're curling back into?
And where is that sigh that created you, that passionate
collision of sperm and egg, the two suddenly
separating, pulling apart
like two countries whose borders are so close,
but will never touch again?

THE WEIGHT OF MY FATHER'S HANDS

They lifted my five-year-old body above the water
of the still glacial lake at dusk,
tossed me into the air so I landed, a bright splash of giggles.
Then he'd point, saying *Look at the way the ripples*
reach all the way to the far shore.

His hands lifted the eight-ounce map of Iowa, traced the branching blue lines
of all the highways he hoped to travel.
They lifted the weight of his tedious sales jobs,
lifted The Miracle Can Opener, boxes of World of Books Encyclopedias,
and bags of feed in tarnished grain elevators,
the kernels of yellow corn spilling through torn seams like smiles.
They lifted a compass and attached it
to the dashboard of his old Chrysler.
That compass weighed more than he thought—
inside its thick liquid bobbed
a needle, and the burden of
intersections—where to turn, where to go forward.

They lifted sixteen-gram packs of green and white Salems,
each one-gram cigarette balanced
between his index and middle fingers.
Though they seemed light at the time, his fingers were lifting
the crushing weight of a heart attack to his lips.

When I left for college, his hands strained under the burden of my future:
What I could possibly do with a life
where I couldn't fix a car but instead filled a page with words?
"Writing poetry is like trying to sell wooden shoes in America," he told me,
a sentence I lugged around with me for years.

When he reached middle age, he gained a hundred pounds,
the red needle on the scale shivering past the 280 mark.
Though Mom asked him to, he refused to step on the scale again.
Those years, he carried the weight of himself around,
rising from the Posturepedic each morning, lifting the feathery
dreams of traveling to South America from his forehead,

dreams that, like monarch butterflies
always fluttered far from his fingertips.

Today I lift a photo of him smiling, leaning
against the blue horizon of his Chrysler.
The photo is thin and faded; it weighs nothing between my fingers,
yet I can barely steady it.
I picture him, slowly crossing the yard for work each morning,
lifting the weight of his whole family, trying to
hold it up, hold it up.
Look, Father: You're in this poem. I've filled this page
with your life, and it weighs
more than you could ever imagine.

For a moment I see his hands hoisting me again
to his broad shoulders,
launching me so I arc in the air and then splash
into the calm lake.
And just like he said they would,
the ripples always reach a long way.

ICE STORMS: LOSING AND FINDING OUR WAY

On the empty highway, our car begins to
spin: Our clear view changes to a
blur as fences and barns rotate around us.
The tires try to grip, but they're bald and
smooth as mercury sliding across glass.

You clutch the chrome door handle
of our car that rotates in the center of the highway, a compass needle
searching the horizon for true north. I see the fear
cracking your face and crank the wheel to the right, as if
following a spin
will make the spin go away.

But the three-sixties continue, one, two, three of them—
and for those moments, we're lost.
I try to call out to you but the words, like corroded wires,
tangle in my throat.
Unsure of what's ahead, both of us duck and cringe, bracing for
the sudden jolt of a post or a tree, or worse—
the fender hitting a guard rail, the car flipping onto its hood,
the two of us trapped inside, staring at the
sky that's suddenly standing on its head.

One hand still on the wheel, I reach
toward you at the same moment you're reaching toward me
until we touch in the middle.
Though the car keeps spinning we don't let go, our
hands clasped so tightly that we memorize each other's fingerprints.
It's those same spiraled fingerprints we recognize the next morning
as we wake and gently touch each other's faces,
grateful as two blind people discovering Braille.
Later, we sip coffee across the table from each other,
amazed that we both had the same nightmare of spinning.
And the more we talk about it,
the more our fear pulls away,
until the ice melts and becomes nothing more than
a water mirage on a highway
disappearing into the horizon.

AFTER SHE'S DIAGNOSED AS LEGALLY BLIND, MY MOTHER REMINISCES IN THE FRONT YARD

Her sight goes gray, opaque moon-like disks on both eyes
and yet she sees:
a picture of herself and her husband—who passed away twelve years ago—
dancing on the square wood tiles of the Elk's Club, Glenn Miller's
caramel-smooth *Moonlight Serenade* making the lights flicker.
Sees the needle she once threaded so easily,
the one she sewed Iowa with, patching it together county by county.
She sees the jagged lines of the pines along the lake,
the first sprinkles of rain ticking against the anxious palms of the oak leaves.

She sees the circus parade she watched as a girl, the red and silver wagons
trundling on spoked wooden wheels, the huge wrinkled backs
of the elephants, washed clean in the river an hour before,
the clown's mouth, forever caught in a smile
too bright for his face. She sees her childhood playground, a wooden swing
creaking on its chains, a spider web
laced like a tightrope between the bars of a jungle gym.
She sees the silence in the river water, the same calm slate-color
no matter how far it flows downstream.

But most of all she sees his hand,
reaching out toward hers, his fingers like the sleek notes of
a clarinet flowing around her late into the night
until the lights dim, and the Elks Club empties
and they're the only couple anchored to the moonlit parquet floor.

"Is it raining?" she asks now. Then she tips her face upward
as though she could see
those tiny clear drops falling all that distance
from the clouds to kiss her open eyes.

WORDS BENEATH THE SKIN: THE SECRET OF THE PENCIL-STAB

1

In fourth grade, when the pencil rolled off the edge of my
desk, I clamped my knees together, trying to catch
it. The graphite point surprised my inner thigh, jabbing
right through my khaki pants. Before I pulled it
out, it stuck there, as if trying to write something beneath my skin.

2

That mark on my thigh never faded,
an unfinished tattoo I couldn't erase from my skin.
I brought it with me through junior high and high school.
The older I got, the lower the spot appeared on my leg,
as if growing up is really growing
down, as if scars fall slowly, steadily toward the earth,
gray shooting stars in slow motion.
It distracted me, yet I learned to accept it—
that bulls-eye, that miniature black hole,
pulling everything in, that tiny, dark mouth always
whispering to me.

3

Years later, I finally understand the secret of the pencil-stab:
Words enter you when you least expect them, at that moment
when you're trying to catch something that's falling.
Sometimes those words
find their way into your bloodstream
and reach all the way to the heart.

I know I'll carry it with me
the rest of my life—that quick bee-sting of pain
which marked me with a small but distinct
dot, that period at the end of a sentence
always stopping me
short, always pushing me
forward toward what I really needed to say.

ORDINARY RAIN: THE GROUNDSKEEPER AT THE END OF THE DAY

Though the deep grass at the edge of the lawn
is about to swallow him, he has to straighten
his small maple, partially
uprooted during last weekend's storm. He cringed
as the winds tore through, quick and
loud as screams, pushing at the flat leaves,
making the trunk slant toward the horizon,
an imperfect angle.

This morning, they left—his wife and teenage daughters
walked out, like they'd threatened. They paused
a moment in the square door frame in their scarves
and their dresses. Always something too short or too long.

He slides on his leather garden gloves, pulls them taut
so there'll be no blisters.
Things have to fit.
He studies the leaning tree,
pushed by the hand of nature
or God or whatever it is that nudges things off
kilter. But it can be

fixed. Everything can be
fixed, he'll tell you. His words are solid,
like the flat field stones he placed edge to sharp edge,
a steady path to the patio.
He bends over, hammering a circle of stakes.
He has to hurry: clouds begin to gather above him,
shrubs still call out to be trimmed,
sharp green weeds need
to have their tongues

pulled out. Lawns must be
mowed and tamed, the clippings dumped, just right,
atop the symmetrical mound of the mulch pile.
His wife just slid into the van, closed the door,

rolled up the fogged window.
She clicked her seat belt and backed out,
the automatic garage door closing behind her, panel by panel,
his two daughters in the back seat,
faces pale as roots,
hunched and staring at their hands.
Go ahead, he told them.
After all, they know nothing about lawns.
Or trees. This evening, on his knees,

he pounds the last wooden stake into the earth's heart, attaches
the taut cords to the tree, straightens
it so the thin trunk points to the center of the mottled sky,
that place from which all rain falls. That place
from which salty drops fall, now,
on the dry soil at the tree's base.
It's rain, he'll tell you, not tears—just the first few drops of
ordinary rain.

SEARCHING FOR A MAP OF THE HOMELAND

When you're lost somewhere on a country road,
strangers will rescue you on the roadside,
wrap you in alfalfa, nurse you on milk
until your cheeks turn creamy.
They'll offer you a place to stay if you admit
the only music you hear
is the flutes of corn stalks in the wind.

You'll notice time slowing down:
in paneled living rooms, minutes are preserved
like rare pennies, collected by elderly men and pressed
into the circular sockets of blue cardboard coin folders.

Soon you, too, will be sitting on the *Furniture Barn* davenport,
staring at *The Reader's Digest* in your underwear.
Soon you, too will begin taking notes during *Unsolved Mysteries,*
and feel a sudden inexplicable yearning
to buy stacks of pull tabs and lottery tickets, to attend a meat raffle.
Soon you'll learn to eat the heartland: plates of tater-tot hot dish,
Jello salad, *Land o' Lakes Butter,* corn grinning ear to ear.
Soon, you'll hear yourself say the sentence "Well, I caught three fish, I suppose"
with this accent: "Whale, I caught tree feesh, I s'pose."

You're never lost again:
you throw away all the maps but one
and promise yourself you'll stay inside the thin blue lines.
And your fingers won't blister, no matter
how hard you press on the paper.

DEATH OF THE VETERAN BASEBALL PITCHER

They never go to hospitals or nursing homes.
They simply stroll to the nearest ballpark,
the rusty chained gates gliding open for them.
They never feel any pain, only the vague ache
of memories: a curve ball someone hit
over the fence, a lost championship game.

They enter the stadium that could be full
of cheering fans. But the seats are
empty—popcorn boxes scuttle across concrete steps.
But the grass, the grass is a color that amazes
the eyes, as if you could grow
a field of green emeralds.

Their cleats barely touch the ground as they
tip their hat to nobody, everybody.
As the wind swirls through the bleachers
they listen to the roar, a roar
so loud it could be
all sound at once, it could be
silence.

In the middle of the diamond, they find a
baseball, its face smooth and clean as a newborn's.
For a moment they feel like they could play
all nine positions at once, they could play for years
without eating or sleeping or ever growing tired.
They lift the ball, cradling it as if it
weighed as much as the whole earth,
then rear back slowly, ready
to throw that first sweet pitch.

MY MOTHER'S OCEAN

I can never take just one photograph of
the ocean. The cerulean waves are too
lovely, too graceful, tumbling gently over themselves,
then turning to foam that kisses
the sandy lip of the world.
There are no other words for it—this
huge and endless ocean's rise and fall, this
rocking back and forth, back
and forth, the way my mother used to

hold me when I was a small child and afraid
of the oncoming storm.
The brittle window glass rattled, but
she rocked me, and replaced the thunder
with a humming, a lullaby
that rose and fell.
It's a melody I would,
as the years passed, remember,
then forget, then
remember again. There are no words

for this song my mother sang, her liquid voice
small, but still filling the room,
overpowering the fists of the wind and stabs of lightning
with a language I couldn't understand

at the time.
One single photograph
is never enough. I know now
that there is beauty in the things that are
closest to us, and beauty in the things
that we lose. She

is gone now.
But as a wave lifts itself and rolls
toward me, then bows down and becomes
a wing of bright diamonds,

I stand again on this shore, without words,
my bare feet sinking into the sand
and wait for that song to wash over me.

THE BASEBALL WIFE AT THE END OF THE SEASON

She's never hit a baseball before,
but when I pitch to her, she swings
and Monarch butterflies rise from the wooden barrel of her bat.
She swings, and sunlight scatters like shards of splintered glass.
Rescued from the bottom of the duffel, my batting gloves
are worn and loose on her hands,
grime darkening the leather palms like storm clouds.
She swings again and the clouds vanish.
Swings once more and oak leaves scatter from the bat,
swings and a Canadian goose arcs gracefully over center,
searching for the flyway south.

"Take a break," I say an hour later, knowing she must be tired.
But she won't step out of the batter's box, crouches there
like she's memorizing every scratched scar on that worn home plate,
levels the bat over it like she's straightening the horizon, waits
for me to toss the next strike.
She'd stay on this diamond until evening,
until it's too dark to see the ball,
her hands learning the resonant song of leather and wood,
wood and leather.

Later, the batting gloves, moist with sweat and exhausted,
curl in the smothered silence of the zipped duffel, wishing for
her slim hands to slide into them again.

In the middle of the night, we lie on a wrinkled field of sheets:
I'd cross a thousand chalk lines to embrace her.
She reaches toward me, her soft, strong arms aching but still dreaming
of just one more swing, one more chance to hit
the moon squarely, shattering it
to luminous pieces, doubling the stars in the night sky.

LAMENT OF THE BROKEN WINDSHIELD

Follow me, I want to say to her, my frantic driver,
though I don't know where I'm going.
I try to see, but my clear, broad eye is spider-webbed,
like paper cuts on tender skin.

The lights pass overhead, always yellow, or
red, or something in between. I can't pause to look. Forward,
I think, before I crack any more, before my sharp pieces
fall onto my driver's dashboard, spill
into her lap and make her bleed,
and make her cry.

My driver believed she could go anywhere, leave
her life behind her with its suffocating corners.
She could go anywhere, she thought, until
the roadmap closed in on her with its wrinkled face,
until a tiny pebble nicked
me, and branching lines suddenly crisscrossed her transparent world.

Now she drives to the other side of the tracks, leaving behind
luring signs for KMartWal-MartTJMaxKohl's,
all the people rushing there, but not her. Instead,
she steers me into a cool, dim mechanic's garage,
where broad glass faces, stacked in piles,
stare at me.

And then I'm lifted out, replaced. Replaced.
It stops her bleeding.
I'm tossed to a pile beside the building, where I cry crystal tears,
and the only thing I can see
are all the cracks in the sky.
Mornings, she drives by, heading toward the edge of town
where the horizon never blinks.
Her vision is so clear again that she never even gives me
a side glance
as she passes.

DANCING WITH THE STARS

Though she's sorting Tupperware in the cupboard,
in her daydream, she's dancing with the stars.

In the yard, hunched over mulch,
he finishes raking the lawn, does a half-spin
toward the front porch, his aching back arching with a Latin flair.

When he enters the doorway of their pale green Glade-scented kitchen
with open-mouthed cupboards
that never seem to close, she asks
When are you ever going to dance with me?

He quick-steps close to her with leather work gloves, bits
of crumbled leaves in his hair.
Cameras, peeking between the seams of the wallpaper, follow them.

Stiff in socks that could be waltzing,
they stumble at first, his Clydesdale foot
clomping her toes, her
kneecaps bumping his, clumsy
on linoleum that will never be a varnished wood stage.

A quick cha-cha change and they're circling each other:
his shoulders shimmying beneath his black silk shirt,
its sheen like the feathers of a grackle or a piece of night sky.
She's doing a mamba in her sudden backless red dress, sequins
sparkling as they catch the attention of the spotlights
and she asks, *When are you ever going to dance with me?*

Near the refrigerator, they slide softly, like melting margarine,
to the left, to the right.
French bread, pasta, and a salad pirouette around a bottle of Merlot.
The two of them are not perfect this round,
her jewelry still waiting to glitter
beneath yellowed fluorescence, his posture a little slumped.
She gently lowers their plates to the table. *When
are you ever going to dance with me?* she asks.

Right now, he replies. In an instant,
the cracked enameled ceiling fills with stars.
He finally takes her in his tango arms and smiles,
leans toward her, pressing the rose in his mouth to her lips.

On the stove, a pan sizzles and snaps
while, in the far corners,
wooden spoons applaud and Ziploc bags sigh.

MY FATHER, THE CONTORTIONIST

My father was a contortionist,
circling his hands until they became
the smooth amber steering wheel of a 1970's Rambler.
He traveled from town to town, bending himself around
a sales pitch for washing machines,
until the whitest shirts rose like genies from that enameled tub.
He hung from a clothesline for a moment, rippling in the breeze
just so customers would see what he meant.

My father was a contortionist, though
there were no sideshows, no gasping audiences: only him,
stretching himself paper-thin as a map
when he followed the endless asphalt roads of central Iowa.
At night, in a run-down motel, he'd disguise himself as
the buzzing neon tubes above the doorway.
Mornings, he'd surprise the sky by stretching his arms
wide as the dawn.

When he'd call home during those weeklong road trips,
Mom held the phone in stiff, shaking fingers
as we three kids crowded around her. We watched as he'd squeezed himself
through a thin black wire and then emerge, large and whole,
right there in our pale green kitchen.
All day his deep voice kept sounding from
the silverware drawer or the dishpan or closet, easing our loneliness.

He was a contortionist, the smile on his lips arcing toward the sky
each time the car broke down, each time he lost a job,
each time he slid his stocky body into a small cardboard box
and somehow moved himself
from rental house to rental house.
P.T. Barnum would have loved him and splashed his image
on a thirty-foot tall canvas poster:
The Astonishing Traveling Salesman!
Be amazed as he spreads his body thin and transparent
as a windshield! the barker with a megaphone would call,
Cheer as he reaches all the way to the horizon and touches it

with his fingertips!
Be astounded *as he drives his old car across the country,*
proving that the earth is flat!
Wonder *as he returns home to circle his thick arms all the way around*
a house with a leaning front porch!
Weep *as he holds a family steady*
for the whole world to see!

And when he steps through the front door, we weep, too,
then embrace him, firmly
but gently, careful not to snap the glass bones
we always knew were inside.

LOSING TIME: MY LAST JOG ON A CARIBBEAN BEACH

The watch slipped from my wrist and dropped
to the sand, burying itself. Retracing
my footprints, I couldn't find it, though I searched
and searched, my palm skimming the beach
like a metal detector.

Home from vacation, I wonder who might
find that watch, wonder
what lonely, homeless beachcomber—years from now—
might idly sift a handful of sand and

discover it. Would the watch be
silent, its cracked face filled with grains that seeped in,
little by little, smothering the two luminous hands?
Or would it still be ticking away in some other time zone,
each sweep of the second hand like a wave
smoothing a distant shore?
If he held it to his ear, like a spiral seashell,
could he hear the azure roar of the ocean inside it?

If I could replace something, it wouldn't be
the watch I lost. Instead, I'd retrieve
a minute, an hour, a day or two, a month,
even a whole year. I'd retrieve
a few friendships, the blurred mistakes I've made,
the faces that faded from the family photo,
an afternoon of tender touching. I'd recover

those moments that passed
while the grains
in the hourglass fell
and fell
in a line so thin and steady I could hardly tell it was moving.

THIS PAGE LEFT INTENTIONALLY BLANK
(After finding six blank pages with this notation in the back of a quarterly financial report)

Or maybe it's filled with what you'd never known was there: a bouquet
of red flowers bursting from the paper,
a waterfall, a palm tree waltzing in the wind.

It's up to you to resurrect a page, adding
the low moan of a whistle as a train trundles across the flatlands,
the yeasty smell of freshly-baked bread in your mother's house,
the taste of the strawberry jam that sweetens your lips,
the kiss of mud oozing between your toes as you
follow a riverbank in spring.

The page bursts with words, thousands, millions
of words that might blur or fade with time,
but are always intentional. Always
intentional. Like grains of sand, they can combine to
create an entire beach,
or the millions of stars arcing above the ocean at night.
Sometimes the words are dark, like drops of blood, sometimes light
and airy, like the lace of snowflakes.

Let nothing be wasted, or left empty. Look:
the clear sky at sunrise paints itself
with scarlet light, then flocks of birds,
then tosses its reflection to the surface of a still lake.
You tip your head back and
the blank page of your face fills and fills
as the first morning breeze writes its daily love letter across it.

ACKNOWLEDGEMENTS/CREDITS

I would like to thank the National Endowment for the Arts, the Loft-McKnight Foundation, and the Minnesota State Arts Board for fellowship awards in poetry. These awards supported the writing of these poems.

I am grateful to the following publications, where these poems appeared:

The Glass Carnival (a chapbook, 2017, Paper Soul Press): "What I Lost on the Way to the Circus: The Love Song of Senorita Rosa," (as "The Love Song of Senorita Rosa"), My Father, the Contortionist," A Day in the Life of a Carnival Princess."
Atlanta Review: "The Propaganda Experts Write Harry Houdini's Eulogy" (winner of an International Publication Award, 2009), nominated for a 2015 Pushcart Prize, and reprinted in *Route Nine*, "Song for the Refugees," "The Ghost of Marilyn Monroe Speaks in the Hollywood Roosevelt Hotel" (winner of an International Publication Award), "The Groundskeeper's Teenage Daughters" (chosen for a 2014 International Poetry Award).
2015 Minnesota Poetry Anthology (Nodin Press): "One Small Explanation of Why I Became a Writer: Words Beneath the Skin," "The Groundskeeper's Teenage Daughters," "A Day in the Life of a Carnival Princess" (reprinted in *The Glass Carnival*), "Solstice Dance in the Village Near Chichen Itza" (reprinted from *Kaleidoscope*), "Baseball Wife at the End of the Season."
North American Review: "Why I Didn't Write the Poem You Asked For."
Notre Dame Review: "The Mapmaker and His Woman."
Margie: "Ten Seconds Left in the High School Championship Game: James Dean Shoots the Basketball from Half Court."
International Poetry Review: "The Things You Carry With You (For the Scar Recovery Therapy Group)" (reprinted in *Route Nine*, 2014).
Great River Review: "To Those Walking Backwards Across America."
Lake Country Journal: "Searching for a Map of the Homeland" (as "Searching for a Map of Minnesota"), "The Weight of My Father's Hands."
New Verse News: "What They Really Want," "A Few Words about Gun Violence: View of the Earth Through the *Dscovr* Telescope," "My Mother's Ocean," "Word by Word."
Studio One: "Lament of the Broken Windshield," "After the Doctors Tell Her She's Legally Blind, My Mother Reminisces in the Front Yard," "A Little Something About the World's Largest Ball of Twine," "The Night Elvis Swallowed His Rosary."
Kaleidoscope: "Solstice Dance in the Village Near Chichen Itza," (reprinted in 2015 *Minnesota Poetry Anthology*), "When the War Vets Return."

Spitball: "Baseball Wife at the End of the Season" (reprinted in 2015 *Minnesota Poetry Anthology).*

Nine: A Journal of Baseball History and Culture: "Death of the Veteran Baseball Pitcher."

Visiting Bob: Poems Inspired by the Life and Work of Bob Dylan (New Rivers Press): "1959: Bob Dylan Hitchhikes on a Country Road Somewhere Outside Hibbing, Minnesota" *Sleet Magazine* published a printed copy and a link to a Youtube video of the poem.

Merida Review: "The Barbie Revolutionaries," "My Father, the Contortionist" (reprinted in *Route Nine,* University of Massachusetts, Amherst, Ma.).

Iconclast: "Mornings Near the End of Winter," "Teenage Boy, Bad at Flowers."

"Song for the Refugees" was chosen as a finalist in the 2018 International Poetry Competition sponsored by the *Atlanta Review.* "My Father, Stalled on the Country Roads" was selected as an International Merit Award winner in the 2018 International Poetry Competition sponsored by the *Atlanta Review.*

Three poems from this collection, "The Propaganda Experts Write Harry Houdini's Eulogy," "1959: Bob Dylan Hitchhikes on a Country Road Somewhere Outside Hibbing, Minnesota," and "The Mapmaker and His Woman" are read by Bill Meissner and set to images and music in videos created by Wayne Nelsen. They are available on Youtube.

James Dean Quote from BrainyQuote.com. Xplore Inc, 2018. 13 April 2018. https://www.brainyquote.com/quotes/james_dean_103528

I am grateful to those who have supported my writing over the years: family, colleagues, former and current students, fellow writers, and friends. The branching map leads to each of you! Thanks to my father and my mother, who taught me to dance beneath the stars while still keeping my feet rooted to the ground.

Most of all, a special thanks to Christine, who guided me through these poems with support and love.

ABOUT THE AUTHOR

Minnesota author and teacher **Bill Meissner's** previous books include four collections of poetry: *American Compass* (U. of Notre Dame Press), *Learning to Breathe Underwater* and *The Sleepwalker's Son* (Ohio U. Press) and *Twin Sons of Different Mirrors*, with Jack Driscoll (Milkweed Editions). His chapbook of poems and short stories is *The Glass Carnival* (Paper Soul Press).

He's also the author of two books of short stories, including *Hitting into the Wind* (Random House Publishers/SMU Press Paperback/Dzanc Press ebook) and *The Road to Cosmos* (U. of Notre Dame Press). His first novel, *Spirits in the Grass* (U of Notre Dame Press), about a small town ball player who discovers the remains of an ancient Native American burial ground on a baseball field, won the Midwest Book Award.

Meissner has won many awards for his poetry, including an NEA Creative Writing Fellowship, a Loft-McKnight Award for Poetry, A Loft-McKnight Award of Distinction in Fiction, a Jerome Fellowship, and a Minnesota State Arts Board Fellowship. His poems have appeared widely in over 350 magazines during the past years.

Three of the poems in *The Mapmaker's Dream* have won national awards sponsored by *The Atlanta Review*, and a poem about Harry Houdini was nominated for a Pushcart Award. Four poems from the collection have been made into videos and are available on Youtube.

Bill's varied part-time jobs and activities during his high school and college years have included: baseball umpire, railroad worker, Circus Museum vendor, city crew worker, radio DJ, garage band member, and creative writing teacher at a home for delinquent youth. His first professional 'writing' job was as a "parts abbreviator" in a warehouse—where his mission was to shorten the descriptions of various hardware items. After receiving an MFA in Creative writing from the University of Massachusetts, he has enjoyed his career as a college creative writing teacher at St. Cloud State University in Minnesota.

Bill's hobbies/interests include travel, rock music, baseball, and photography. He also collects pulp fiction magazines, music memorabilia, and (too many) vintage typewriters. He frequently presents workshops at local elementary schools, high schools and colleges as a visiting writer.

He lives with his wife, Christine, in St. Cloud, Minnesota, though they travel widely throughout the year, including recent trips to Mexico, Costa Rica, Puerto Rico, Quebec City, Vancouver, Hawaii, and the U.S. Virgin Islands.

His Facebook author page is https://www.facebook.com/wjmeissner/

CPSIA information can be obtained
at www.ICGtesting.com
Printed in the USA
LVHW091752060619
620403LV00054B/849/P

9 781635 348316